skin

and other
teenage reflections

Illustrated by Scott Byers

Poems by

Angela Shelf Medearis

WingsPress

San Antonio, Texas

2013

Skin Deep and other teenage reflections © 1995, 2005, 2014
by Angela Shelf Medearis

Pen & ink illustrations by Scott Byers © 1997 by Diva Productions
Cover illustration & book design by Bryce Milligan.

Second, slightly revised Wings Press Edition
(Originally published in 1995 by Diva Productions, Austin, Texas)

Printed Edition ISBN: 978-1-60940-363-8
ePub ISBN: 978-1-60940-364-5
Kindle ISBN: 978-1-60940-365-2
Library PDF ISBN: 978-1-60940-366-9

(Replaces ISBN 0-9660873-0-5 and/or 0-916727-22-X)

Wings Press
627 E. Guenther
San Antonio, Texas 78210
Phone/fax: (210) 271-7805
On-line catalogue and ordering:
www.wingspress.com

Library of Congress Cataloging-in-Publication data:
Skin Deep and other teenage reflections / by Angela Shelf
Medearis
  p.   cm.
  ISBN 978-1-60940-363-8 (pbk. : alk. paper) -- ISBN 978-1-
60940-364-5 (epub) -- ISBN 978-1-60940-365-2 (mobipocket
ebook) -- ISBN 978-1-60940-366-9 (pdf ebook)
1. Title. 2. Teenagers–Poetry. 3. Young adult poetry.
[1. Adolescence–Poetry. 2. American poetry.]
Byers, Scott, ill.
PS3563.E2384S58   2014
811'.54–dc20

For more information about Angela Shelf Medearis:
www.divapro.com

To my darling daughter
Deanna Renee,
my source of inspiration for this book,
and for teenagers everywhere,
especially Anysa Renee.
Hang in there.
Love,
Angela Shelf Medearis

REPORT CARD

-⋀⋀-

I'd have an A in algebra
or even a good passing
B
or even a "tried but couldn't quite make it"
C
if good-looking you
weren't seated right next to me.

What Would I Do Without You?

-⋀⋀-

What would I do without you?
My friend. My best friend.
You're as close
(sometimes closer)
to me than my own family.
You know all my secrets,
and you never tell.
You held my hand when I thought I
was going to lose my mind,
bought my lunch
with your last dollar,
loaned me your favorite
shirt and stayed mad only
for a little while when I lost it.
You always find something about me to love,
even when I can't find anything
to love about myself.
My friend. My best friend.
What would I do without you?
I don't even want to think about it.

I'd Rather

I'd rather walk
over a bed of hot coals
with my bare feet
through a jungle
with snakes dripping off of every tree
and lie on a bed of
carefully sharpened nails
with a 2,000 pound weight on
my chest
than walk through the hall
where all the boys hang out.

Jigsaw

I've been trying so hard to
fit in
that I've lost
parts of myself.

Maintaining an Attitude

-⋀⋀⋀-

I'm having a hard time being cool
posing and
maintaining the right attitude
with
her around.

Friendship

-⋀⋀⋀-

When your two best friends are arguing
and you're right in the middle,
it's best to be friends
with yourself.

Skin Deep

-MM-

I wish my skin came
equipped with a zipper
right in the center of my belly button.
Then,
when I see the fear creep into your eyes
and your mind fill up with
all those things your momma told you
and the newspapers told you
and you saw on the TV or heard on the radio
about BLACK people
ZIPPPPPP
I could slip out of my skin.
I'd look just like those pictures in an
anatomy book,
red and blue veins everywhere.
Just another naked human being,
no different than you.

The Bogeyman

-///-

My mother used to tell me about the bogeyman
so I would stay in bed at night.
But since I ran away from home
and started living on the streets
I've met the *real*
BOGEYMAN.
I wish I was back home
in my own bed.

The Oldest

-⋀⋀-

After years of cold, unexplained silences
and electric tension
my parents are getting a divorce.
Since I'm
the oldest,
they told me first
so I can help explain it to
my little brothers and sisters.
My only question is,
who's going to explain it
to me?

You Have My Deepest Sympathy
As You Go Through Puberty

-⋀⋀⋀-

Your voice shifted between middle G, low F,
and an ear-piercing high C
in just one sentence.
Your body is in a hairy revolt.
You cry and laugh
and laugh and cry
within the space of five minutes.
Your emotions are a roller coaster
of feelings
too hard to express
and too painful to forget.
Your mind is a jumble of weird thoughts
with no explanations,
and no one really understands you.
If they did, they wouldn't leave you so alone.
But, maybe solitude is a good thing
because your face is a mess anyway.
Insanity?
No, puberty. PUBERTY.
Radical changes in your mind and body
without your consent.
Cheer up,
there are survivors
of this dreaded
disease
they're called . . .
ADULTS.

Prescription

-⅄⅄-

Dad drinks to relax.
Mom has a pill for every occasion –
red ones, yellow ones, blue ones,
a pharmaceutical rainbow.
Me? I dabble in a little of this
and a lot of that.
We're all doing something.
So why am I the one who's
committed to this institution?

Modern Dating

-⋀⋀-

I saw her today in the hallway.
She was standing by her locker.
I only had a few minutes
to ask her that important question.
"Hi," I said.
"Hi," she said.
"Look," I said. "Um, um, uh . . ."
"Do you want to go to the dance?" she said.
"Yeah," I said.
"That's great," she said. "I'll see you later."
"Yeah," I said.
Oh well, I guess I can borrow her history notes
some other time.

Dressing Out

-ᴧᴧᴧ-

I would rather have the mumps than
dress out for gym.
I never wanted to be physically fit anyway.
The worst part about gym
is the stupid gym suits you have to wear.
The tag inside says
"one size fits all,"
all but me I guess.
I look like a baby-blue Polish sausage in that thing.
Just when I figured I'd have straight F's
in physical fitness,
the school board decided to revoke the
rule about wearing gym suits.
Yeahhh!
Of course, I still look like a Polish sausage
in my shorts,
but at least I have a choice.

Boys

-⟋⟋⟍-

BOYS,
BOYS, BOYS, BOYS,
BOYS, BOYS, BOYS, BOYS, BOYS, BOYS,
that's all I think about!
I'm going to get a new hobby
just as soon as I have time
to think about something besides
BOYS.

Lunchroom

-⟋⟋⟍-

I was so hungry
I could have eaten my algebra book.
I smelled what we were having
before I even saw it.
Mystery Meat, green mushy peas,
instant potatoes with lumpy gravy,
bread pudding, and milk.
It's a good thing I like milk.

My Mirror Lies to Me

-ᴍᴍ-

My mirror lies to me,
it whispers,
YOU ARE FAT, FAT, FAT.

I starve myself into
skeletal thinness to
the alarm of my loved ones,
crumbs fill me up like a Thanksgiving feast
and are purged from my
stomach with medicines.

I stick my finger down
my throat after a meal
of half of a half of a cracker
and yet,
my mirror still whispers FAT, FAT, FAT.

I've almost killed myself in the pursuit
of perfection,
only to find out that
what I'm really starving for
is love.

Poem For My Little, Big Sister

-ᴧᴧ-

When I want to be wise,
I pretend that I am you.
I smile, listen carefully,
and keep my mouth shut.
When I'm feeling defeated,
I think of you,
the way that you always persevere,
finish what you start,
and triumph in adversity.

When I'm down,
I hum the songs you sing so well,
and when I want to smile,
I conjure up the crazy way you laugh
when you think something is funny.
My little, big sister.
I really love you.
You lead so well,
I don't mind following you at all.

Black Barbie Doll

-MM-

I'm tired of you calling me a
black barbie doll
because most of my friends are white
and I get good grades
and I talk "proper,"
whatever that means.
This is me, this is how I want to be.
Nobody is going to squeeze me into
a box labeled
black or white.
Okay?

The Blemish

-ΛΛΛ-

I have a pimple on my right cheekbone.
IT'S HUGE!
It glows red in the light
and blinks off and on in
the dark.
It sings a little song that only I can hear,
"You can't pop me, uh huh!"
It feels like it covers
my whole face.
All my friends claim
it's not that noticeable,
but then,
I'm wearing two pounds
of makeup.
For days, it was all I
could think about
until
another one appeared . . .

on

the end

of my nose!

Nonconformist

-ᐧᐧᐧ-

I don't want to be anybody
but myself.
So, I shaved little lines
in my head and
dyed my hair purple
and green
(with just a hint of orange)
and pierced my nose and
hung a gold earring in it,
AS AN EXPRESSION OF WHO I AM
(who am I?).
Of course,
I waited until someone else did it first.
I didn't want anyone to think I'm
weird.
You know what I mean?

The Gang

-⋀⋀-

We were together when we got high.
We were together when we stole the car.
We were together when we did the crime.
We were together when we got caught.
But I'm serving this life sentence all alone.

Pea Brain

-⋀⋀-

At our school
it's cool to be
stupid.
I don't tell anyone
I make straight A's.
I don't know why
most guys prefer to think
that your brain is
the size of a pea.
Can I help it if
my name is permanently
engraved on
the honor roll?

In the Bathroom Mirror

-ΛΛΛ-

In the bathroom mirror
I am transformed.
Sometimes,
I have muscles that pop out like THE HULK's.
Sometimes,
I'm a secret agent trained in karate.
My chops and kicks look great
in the bathroom mirror.
Sometimes,
I'm Kool Baby Kool,
the rock star,
master of the air guitar.
When I play
the chicks swoon and sway
and scream my name
and . . .
this daydream has been temporarily interrupted.
My little sister is screaming at me
because she has to use the bathroom.
Okay! Okay, I'm coming out.

Sunglasses

-ᏘᏘᏘ-

I wear these dark glasses
because they're really cool
(and because I don't want you to see
the fear
in my eyes.)
I walk like I do
because
I'm trying to keep
from running.
I try to stay alive with a rap
style that drives 'em wild
with what I say each and every day
because
no one seems to
understand me
when I'm talking anyway.

Mom Says

-ᴧᴧ-

Mom says
"Be careful!"
"Where are you going?"
"What time are you coming home?"
I say
"I know what I'm doing!"
"Quit treating me like I'm a baby!"

I guess we keep telling each other
the same old things
in the same old way
because
we're too scared to say
I love you.

I Was Born at the Wrong Time

-/\/\/\-

I had to ask
my mom
to define
a "sit-in".
You know, they sit in a place
to protest something,
carry signs, and get arrested.
I had to ask about it
because I was born at the wrong time.
All the excitement is over with.
My mom had already marched for civil rights,
sung WE SHALL OVERCOME,
shouted BLACK POWER,
MARCHED ON WASHINGTON,
had a basketball-sized Afro,
sang sweet soul music,
and cried over
Martin Luther King Jr. and both Kennedys
long before my first birthday.
I wonder if there will be any causes left
to believe in
by the time I'm old enough
to join in the fight?

Forever

-⋀⋀-

You told me that we were going
to be together
forever.
You said that I was yours
and you were mine
forever.
You said that you were going
to love me
forever.
I wish you would have told me that
forever
is only
three months long.

Binky

-⋀⋁⋀-

My mom cleaned my room yesterday.
I didn't notice anything important was missing
until that night.
She threw away Binky!
How could she throw Binky away?
I know he was leaking stuffing,
and one ear was missing
(I cut it off when I was pretending to be a doctor),
and his white fur had turned
a pale shade of gray,
but he's mine and I love him.
I can't sleep without him.
I crept downstairs with a flashlight
and went outside.
There was Binky, sitting on the trash heap.
I rescued him and crept back upstairs.
I slept great,
and so did Binky.
From now on, I'm hiding him in the closet.

Tryouts

-⁀MM⁀-

This is the most important day
of my entire life.
Cheerleader tryouts.
I've practiced until I'm
practically hoarse.
I've bounced, done the splits,
turned cartwheels, and
smiled until all my
muscles froze
in one huge cramp.
I had to bathe in liniment.
Oh no, they're calling my name.
Where are my pom-poms?
YEAAAH, TEAMMMMMM!

Gray

-⋀⋁⋀-

All the color has left the world,
Everything is black and white,
I can't tell night from day,
Or decipher day from night.
Nothing is funny anymore,
Life is just routine.
I don't want to bathe or change my clothes
I like not being clean.

I don't know how long I've been this way,
or how things were before.
I'm locked and chained inside myself
in a room without windows or doors.
I'm in the deepest pit of despair,
and the walls are too smooth to climb out.
I'm begging for help
in my own way
in a whisper that sounds like a shout.

A Whole New Look

-⋏⋏⋀-

I got my braces taken off on Tuesday.
I got my hair cut and a curly perm on Wednesday.
I got contacts on Thursday.
Friday when I went to school
no one knew who I was.

Wait for Me

-⋏⋏⋀-

The world is full of trash,
the government is running out of cash,
people sleep in the streets
like the pavement is their
own private bedroom.
A nuclear bomb will probably kill us all
before I can get my driver's license.
But I haven't given up hope.
If I can just get out of high school
I'm going to change the world.

Career Day

-MM-

Tables of smiling adults
with brochures about
engineering, medical technology,
law school, teaching, and
hundreds of jobs of all types.
Nothing
appealed to me.
Does this mean
that I'm going to make a career
out of doing nothing?

I Haven't Really Thought About It

-MM-

Why is it that adults always ask you
the same question
in different ways?
"What are you going to do when you grow up?"
"Decided on a career yet?"
How can I plan a lifetime
when I haven't even decided
what I want to wear tomorrow?

Innocent

-ᐱᐱ-

If love were a crime,
and you were jailed because you claimed that you love
me,
and evidence was sought of your guilt or innocence,
You'd get away scott free.

Feelings Left Unspoken

-ᐱᐱ-

If my heart could speak,
would you then be able to comprehend it?
Better feelings left unspoken
than to be destroyed by the truth.

Immune

-⋏⋏⋎-

I am young.
Therefore,
I am immune
to
AIDS
WAR
CANCER
AND OTHER DEADLY
ILLNESSES
and those WEIRD THINGS that happen to
other people
on TV.
I am young, and
strong, and alive.
Nothing can happen to me.
The only thing I haven't figured out is . . .
why do they make
coffins
in different sizes?

Safety

-∿-

I'm really kind of afraid to graduate.
I feel safe in high school.
Who knows what will happen when all this is over?
They allow you to screw up when you're just a kid.
It's sort of expected of you.
But they don't make allowances
for adults.

Guilty Until Proven Innocent

-∿-

When you see me,
you cross the street.
You follow me around
so much that the
real criminals get away.
My skin is the only
search warrant you'll ever need.
What's the point in
trying to be correct,
when no matter what I do
I look wrong to you?

The Test

-ᨇᨇ-

I passed the written part just fine.
I practically had the whole book memorized.
I knew when to yield, when to stop, how to signal,
and all that stuff.
Then came the driver's test.
I was so nervous I could barely hold the wheel.
The officer who was riding with me
was a big guy with a big gun.
I wonder if he shoots you if you make an illegal turn?
Everything was going pretty good,
but then he asked me to parallel park.
I hate parallel parking. I can never get it right.
I gave him a sickly grin.
He didn't smile, he just rubbed the handle of his gun.
That was the best parallel parking I've ever done.
It's amazing what you can do
when you're under pressure.

Babies

-WW-

I wanted a baby because
I wanted something of my very own
to love.
I never thought I'd have twins.
I didn't know how much little,
helpless babies need you.
Day and night, night and day,
it seems like I'm climbing a
mountain of disposable diapers.
All I do is sterilize bottles
and wipe butts.
I never have fun anymore.
Who wants a double date with a couple of infants?

Moving On

-⋀⋀-

I traded my baseball cap for a cap and gown,
Nikes for a pair of leather dress shoes,
jeans for slacks,
and my warm up jacket for a sports coat.
I looked in the mirror and hardly recognized
myself.

I've packed most of the stuff in my room,
and today, I'm headed off for college.
But it's all good.
Everything is different on the outside,
but I'm still the same me on the inside.

I'm Not Jealous

-ΛΛΛ-

I'm not jealous of my sister,
I'm really not.
I think it's great that she's
so little and cute
(although when we stand side by side
I look like Godzilla).
Just because her hair and clothes
are always perfect
(and I always look like an unmade bed)
and she makes nothing lower than an A
(and I rejoice over C's)
and people always say in that
disbelieving tone of voice,
"Are you really sisters?!?"
It doesn't make me jealous.
Not at all, not one little bit.
Really, it doesn't.
I AM NOT JEALOUS!

Chemical Cocoon

-↯↯↯-

Every morning, I carefully wrap myself up
in a chemical cocoon.
I don't want to feel anything
I don't want to hear anything
I don't want to learn anything new.
I know enough about this old world.
It's nothing but a big ball of pain.
Maybe, one of these days
I'll emerge from all this
whole and beautiful
just like a butterfly.
If I live that long.

I'm Going to Be Homecoming Queen Even If It Kills Me

-↯↯↯-

I've spent the last two weeks
being nice to everybody,
even that gross guy
in my third period class.
This is my last chance to be
HOMECOMING QUEEN.
Every vote counts.
It's so hard to be nice
when you're really not.

The Basket

-ʌʌʌ-

I've been sitting on the bench almost the whole season.
Finally, the coach sent me in.
Some big guy practically mopped the court with me
so the referee called a foul.
He threw the ball to me so I could shoot.
My big moment. My big chance.
I was a sweaty mess.
I bounced the ball until someone yelled
"So shoot it already!"
I gripped the ball tightly
and pumped it up through the air.
The ball landed gently on the rim of the basket,
and slid through the net. YES!
I know, it was the last ten seconds of
the final quarter,
and we were leading 110 to 66 anyway.
But it was the most important shot of the game
to me.

Colors of the Race

-⋀⋀⋀-

So, you finally found out what I knew all along.
My big full lips are beautiful
and so envied that
you pay
to have yours plumped up.
Roller coaster curves
and caramel cream to deep ebony skin tones
show off clothes to perfection.
Let's not even talk about
all the ways I can style my hair,
previously labeled as
"nappy."
Yeah, sometimes I might be loud
and unafraid to speak up for myself,
but I was raised to be proud,
no need to whisper,
or smile falsely.
I'm glad you finally realize
that all the colors of the race
are beautiful.

Me and You

-ΛΛΛ-

The difference between me and you,
is that while you talk,
I do.
While you contemplate life,
I live it.
When you withhold love,
I give it.
What you cast away,
I value.
And while you stay at home,
I travel.
When you hesitate,
I follow through.
Who enjoys life most:
me or you?

Say That Again?

-ΛΛΛ-

Like, you broke up with me
because you said that
your parents said that
we are too young
to be so serious about each other.
Since you love, love, love, love me, and will never
ever forget me,
why are you dating her?